SCHOLASTIC'S
A+ JUNIOR GUIDE
TO BOOK REPORTS

Other A+ Junior Guides for you

Scholastic's A+ Junior Guide to Good Writing
by Louise Colligan
Scholastic's A+ Junior Guide to Studying
by Louise Colligan

SCHOLASTIC'S A+ JUNIOR GUIDE TO BOOK REPORTS

LOUISE COLLIGAN

SCHOLASTIC INC.
New York Toronto London Auckland Sydney

ISBN 0-590-42148-4

12 11 10 9 8 7 6   0 1 2 3 4/9

Printed in the U.S.A.   28

First Scholastic printing, January 1989

To Deirdre, Kelly, Marisa, Melissa, and Molly,
the A+ Girls

Table of Contents

1
Help, I've Got a Book Report Due! What Do I Do First?

Do you think writing a book report is the surest way to ruin a good book? Are you afraid you'll not only pick the wrong book but have to write about it, too? Or that you won't be able to think of enough to say to fill out all those pages your teacher wants?

Many middle schoolers feel exactly the same way. Like you, they wonder why they can't just curl up with a good book, read it, enjoy it, and return it to the library. For most students, writing a book report is right up there with cleaning their rooms. What's the point of book reports, anyway?

The point is that book reports are not only about books, they are about you, too. What you think about books matters to the people who care about your opinions — your teachers, your classmates, and your family. Writing a book report helps you express your opinions and back them up. The thinking you do when you plan a book report helps

1

you get more out of a book than just reading it would.

Good writers spend a lot of time writing books. Some writers will rewrite one sentence a dozen times before they are satisfied. Reading a book for a book report helps you slow down long enough to appreciate the writer's special touches. Thinking about the characters, seeing how the story works out, then going and studying how a book was put together will make you a better reader.

If book reports still make you feel as if you're coming down with the flu, maybe you're one of those people who tries to do it all at once — the reading, notetaking, writing, and rewriting. If you have been hoping for a better way to survive book reports, try the following steps instead.

Ten Steps to A + Book Reports

Think about what happens when you get ready to act in a class play, sing in a school concert, or play in a big game. Don't you usually practice a little, do a few warm-ups, and spend a few weeks getting ready? Any project, including book reports, will go more smoothly when you work on it regularly and in small doses. So instead of thinking of a book report as a huge, all-or-nothing assignment that's going to ruin your life until it's done, tell yourself you are going to do the job a step at a time, the way you would any other kind of project. Ten small steps spread out over a couple of weeks will lead you to a super report and still give you plenty of time to play soccer and hang out with your friends. Here is how to turn that big job you may be worried about into a manageable series of small jobs:

Prewriting

Step 1: Write down everything you need to know about the assignment.

Step 2: Visit the library or bookstore right away and choose at least two books.

Step 3: Plan a daily reading and writing schedule.

Step 4: Read a little every day.

Step 5: Take notes as you read.

Step 6: Organize your notes.

Writing

Step 7: Write your first draft.

Revising and Editing

Step 8: Revise and proofread your first draft.

Step 9: Recopy your paper into a final draft.

Step 10: Turn your paper in on the due date.

To come up with your best book report ever, let's take a closer look at how to accomplish the work in each of these steps.

Prewriting

Step 1: Write down everything you need to know about the assignment.

Word for word, write down everything your teacher tells you. If you're lucky enough to get a handout sheet instead, put it right into your notebook. Then, before you leave class, make sure you can answer these questions:

• *What type of book are you supposed to write about?* Does your teacher want you to choose books from a special list? Can you choose fiction (made-up stories, novels, plays, poems) or nonfiction (books about real life)? Many teachers like to have students report on at least one biography each year. Find out just what sort of book your teacher expects you to read.

• *What is the report supposed to include?* Does your teacher expect you to write a plot summary, your opinion, or both? Are you supposed to turn in artwork as well? Does your teacher want an oral report or a written one? Do you have to put a cover on the report? Get answers to these and any other questions you have before you leave class. If you are still confused, talk to your teacher or a classmate right after class.

• *What is the due date?* Have you ever seen two or three weeks shrink down to two days in no time? If you're like most students, this sometimes happens when you get a longer-than-usual project that is due in a few weeks. You get the assignment, and it seems as if you have *ages* to do it. Then life gets in the way — piano lessons, a movie, Scout meetings, Little League practice, and before you know it, you wind up with a few days left to do a big job. This happens to everyone once in a while. The cure is this. Write down your due date both in your homework pad and wherever you keep track of appointments and deadlines at home, say, on a wall calendar in your room or in the kitchen. Write your deadline in BIG LETTERS so you can't miss it.

Step 2:   Visit the library or bookstore right away and choose at least two books.

Another part of the putting-off-until-tomorrow cure is to get your books immediately, even sooner, if possible! This way, you will get first crack at the most popular books *and* give yourself an early boost that will make you feel your book report is really underway.

Why pick at least two books? Backup books will give you alternatives to getting stuck with a boring book. Writing a report on a book you like will be a lot easier than reporting on one you can't get into. Chapter 2 is filled with tips on how to choose the books that are just right for you.

Step 3:   Plan a daily reading and writing schedule.

Set aside one third of the time you have for writing the report. Then divide up the rest of the time by the number of pages or chapters in your book. For example, if your book report deadline is three weeks away, give yourself 14 reading days at the beginning and leave yourself a week at the end to write your paper. A book of 150 pages, say, divided by 14 means you would have to read about 10 pages a day.

Some students prefer reading chapter by chapter. A 28-chapter book divided by 14 would require you to read about 2 chapters a night, which is a manageable dose for most readers. In your daily assignment pad, write down READ where you put your homework notes in other subjects.

Step 4: Read a little every day.

Once you have your schedule worked out, plan to read your assigned pages or chapters each day no matter what. If you fall behind, double up the next day so that you get right back on track. Bring the book with you everywhere and dip into it whenever you get a chance — on the school bus, at the orthodontist's, or during study period. Or set aside a fixed reading time every day — during study period, when you get home, or before bed. Do nothing else but read your book at that time. No matter where and when you read, if you've picked the right book, you may even get ahead of schedule. Be the first kid on Planet Earth to get a book report done *early!*

Steps 5 and 6:   Takes notes as you read, and organize them.

Taking notes as you go along is the surest way of doing the hardest part of a book report in a painless way. Here's what you do. Get a sheet of notebook paper. Copy the following information on each side of the sheet. Fold the sheet in half. You now have a great bookmark for your book and a handy place to take notes as you go along. If you really want to get ahead on future book reports, see if you can get someone in your family to make copies of this blank form to have on hand for every book report you write. You will find that taking notes on this form will help you plan out your report ahead of time and get you in gear for writing.

Use one form for fiction books and one for nonfiction. For samples of bookmark note sheets, see pages 8-11 and pages 64-67 in Chapter 5.

```
┌─────────────────────────────────────────────────┐
│                  (Side 1)                       │
│            BOOKMARK NOTE SHEET                   │
│                  Fiction                        │
├─────────────────────────────────────────────────┤
│   Title:                                        │
├─────────────────────────────────────────────────┤
│   Author:                                       │
├─────────────────────────────────────────────────┤
│ ◯ Date Book Was Published:                      │
├─────────────────────────────────────────────────┤
│                                                 │
├─────────────────────────────────────────────────┤
│   1. Summary                                    │
│         Main Characters:                        │
│         Name            A few words about them  │
│                                                 │
│                                                 │
│                                                 │
│                                                 │
├─────────────────────────────────────────────────┤
│ ◯       Plot:                                   │
│         The book begins when                    │
│                                                 │
│                                                 │
│         Most of the story takes place (when and where) │
│                                                 │
│                                                 │
│         The main events and problems that happen are │
│ ◯                                               │
│                                                 │
│         The story ends when                     │
│                                                 │
│                                                 │
└─────────────────────────────────────────────────┘
```

(Side 1)

BOOKMARK NOTE SHEET

Fiction

Title:

Author:

◯ Date Book Was Published:

1. Summary

Main Characters:

Name   A few words about them

◯ *Plot:*

The book begins when

Most of the story takes place (when and where)

The main events and problems that happen are

The story ends when

(Side 2)

2. Author's Main Idea

     I think the author was trying to say that

     Page numbers of quotations that show the author's
main idea:

3. Special Feature

     One part of the book that makes it special (or weakens
it) is

     Page numbers of quotations that show this special
feature:

4. Your Opinion

     This book made me feel that

     I would ___ would not ___ recommend this book because

     Other page numbers I might need:

(Side 1)

BOOKMARK NOTE SHEET

Nonfiction

Title:

Author:

◯ Date Book Was Published:

1. Summary

   This book is about

2. Author's main idea

   The author thinks that

   ◯

   Page numbers of quotations that show the author's

   main idea:

3. Special feature

   ◯ One of the good/bad things about this book is that

   Page numbers of quotations or examples that show

   special feature:

10

(Side 2)

4. Opinion

This book helped me learn that

○ _____

_____

_____

I would ___ would not ___ recommend this book because

_____

_____

_____

Other page numbers I might need:

○ _____

_____

_____

_____

_____

_____

○ _____

_____

_____

_____

_____

11

2
Choosing a Great Book

If you saw these two titles on a bookshelf, which would you choose: *The Dog Who Came to Stay* or *The Alien Who Came to Stay*? When you pick a television show or movie to watch, are you more likely to choose a family comedy or an adventure? Something that features a crime or a haunted house? A movie that makes you laugh or one that requires a box of tissues by your side? Do you go for believable stories about kids your age or programs that feature laser weapons and space-age vehicles?

Reading a book on a subject you like makes the job of writing a book report easy and fun. So even if you have a required reading list, find out which books on the list are about subjects you like already or wish you knew more about. A 90-page book that makes you yawn will seem a lot longer than a 200-page book about something you are interested in.

There are so many books to choose from, how

can you tell which ones would be fun to read?

• Borrow or swap favorite books with your friends and classmates. Books that kids your age have bought or saved usually make great reading.

• Ask older kids what books they liked reading at your age. Have them look at any class book list you have and ask them to check off books they remember liking (or wish they had avoided).

• What books do the grown-ups in your life remember loving? Some adults — maybe your parents, aunts, uncles, grandparents, teachers, and school librarians — still remember wonderful details in books from the *Little House on the Prairie* or *The Chronicles of Narnia* series. If someone still remembers a book fondly after many years, there's a good chance it will be special for you, too.

• Young adult and children's librarians know exactly which books students your age check out over and over again. If you let the librarian know a little bit about yourself and the kinds of books you have liked in the past, he or she can suggest titles tailor-made for you.

• Readers can never get enough of their favorite authors. Is there an author whose book or books you already enjoyed? Try a third or fourth book by that author. You might even want to consider writing a report in which you compare several of that author's books.

• Do you wish you knew more about snakes,

juggling, pioneers, baseball heroes, or science fiction? Think about using your book report assignment as a way of introducing yourself to a new, interesting subject. Again, your librarian can help you pick the best book in the field.

• Do check in with your teacher to let him or her know which titles you are considering for your book report if they are not on the class book list. While you might think that *The Monster That Ate Green Slime* sounds like a great book, your teacher may not agree.

Check It Out:
Finding the Books You Want in the Library

Some readers track down good books just by walking up and down the library stacks looking for a title, an author's name, or a book jacket that catches their attention. Other readers watch for books that the librarians put on special display — new books, a collection of one author's books, books grouped by a special theme or holiday, old favorites the librarians want you to know about. You can find some terrific books in such displays, particularly if the grouping is about a subject you like.

Sometimes, though, you have to dig around a little more to find the book that will be just right for you. The more comfortable you feel in the library, the better your chances of finding the perfect book.

The best guide to the best books is your librarian. Sometimes students feel shy about approaching the librarian, who may be busy checking out books, stacking them, typing, answering the phone, and so on. Keep in mind that for most librarians, the best part of their job is helping young readers like you choose just the right book.

See if you can catch the librarian at a quiet time and introduce yourself. Mention that you have a book report due soon and would like a recommendation of a few good books. Let the librarian know what kinds of books you have liked before, and what your hobbies and interests in movies and television are. Show the librarian your class reading list and ask him or her to point out some titles that you might like. Then see if you can locate these books yourself. If you aren't sure how to find the books you want, here's a quick rundown of the way most libraries are organized:

• *Fiction* titles are located in their own section of the library. These books are shelved *alphabetically* by the *author's last name*. That means that a book by Astrid Lindgren will come after one by C.S. Lewis but before a book by Lois Lowry.

• *Nonfiction* titles are grouped on the nonfiction shelves by *subject*. For example, nonfiction books about outer space will be together on the nonfiction

15

shelves; so will animal, vegetable, and mineral books. Biographies and autobiographies have their own section near the nonfiction area.

• *Reference* books like encyclopedias, atlases, and fact guides are in a third area of the library. These books can't be taken out of the library, but are great to use if you have to look up specific facts quickly and don't want to read a whole book on the subject. While you probably won't be using reference books for a book report, many libraries do have book guides in the reference section to help readers find out a little information about a lot of good books.

Many libraries keep a copy of a reference book that describes the best books for students your age: *Your Reading, a Booklist for Junior High and Middle School Students*, published in 1983 by the National Council for Teachers of English.

The Children's Book Council publishes a yearly booklet called *Children's Choices*, which lists recent books that students from all over the country have read and recommended. From time to time, this organization also publishes a bookmark that lists annual Newbery Medal winners. This is a prize for the best book written each year for readers your age. Ask your librarian if he or she has one of these useful booklets or bookmarks.

Once you know what book you want to read,

how do you locate it without walking up and down the aisles?

• Check the *card catalogue*. This is a cabinet that contains a file card for every fiction and nonfiction book in that library. The cabinet is divided into three sections of file drawers under *Title*, *Author*, and *Subject*. Say you want to read a book about the stars. There are three ways you could find a book on that subject. In the *Subject* section, flip through alphabetical cards labeled ASTRONOMY or STARS in the upper left corner of the card. There you might find this subject card:

STARS

J   Rey, Hans Augustus

523.8   Find the Constellations;

R   Houghton, 1962, 72 pp., illus.

        1. Astronomy 2. Stars

The Dewey Decimal number on the side indicates the aisle and shelf location of this nonfiction book and others on the same subject.

Now suppose you have read other books by

Hans Rey and want to try another. To see what other books Rey has written, go to the *Author* section of the card catalogue and look up this author's last name alphabetically. The *Author* card would look like this:

```
J          Rey, Hans Augustus
523.8      Find the Constellations
R          Houghton, 1962, 72 pp. illus.

           1. Astronomy   2. Stars
```

Say your best friend recommends just the title, *Find the Constellations*. How would you locate it? Go to the *Title* section of the catalogue and find the *Title* card there. The card will look like the one on page 19 and lists the call number that tells you exactly where on the shelves this title is located.

```
J          Find the Constellations
523.8      Rey, Hans Augustus
R          Find the Constellations
           Houghton, 1962, 72 pp., illus.
           1. Astronomy  2. Stars
```

Some libraries use microfiche machines instead of card catalogues. Information for fiction is listed under *Title* and *Author*, just as in the card catalogue; nonfiction books are arranged under *Subject*, *Author*, and *Title*. However, instead of appearing on cards, these entries are listed on microfilm sheets which the user inserts into a microfiche machine. Ask your librarian to show you how to use the microfiche machine if you don't know how yet.

Once you know your way around the library, check out at least two books you might want to read for your report. When you get home, read the first ten or fifteen pages of one right away to see if you like it. If not, switch to one of the other books you brought home.

Read All About It:
Getting the Most From Your Reading

Do you have to read a book differently just because you are going to write a book report about it? It is important to read a book report book a little more carefully than you would if you were reading a book at the beach. To come up with a good book report, you will need to get in the habit of noticing and thinking about certain parts of the book. That's where the bookmark note sheets shown in Chapter 1 come in handy.

As you read, stop every now and then to fill in information about the plot, characters, and setting. This will help you notice how the author put the book together. After you have read a few books this way, you will be able to move along fairly quickly and still have all the information at your fingertips when you get ready to write.

Reading Fiction

For many students, fiction is a welcome change of pace from the factual information they study in math, science, and social studies. There's something relaxing and a little fantastic about losing yourself in a world where all the people, places, and events are both believable and imaginary.

The following are special features of a novel that you should know about.

Plot: the chain of events in a story. When you tell somebody what a movie, television program, or book is about, you are describing its *plot*.

Character: the imaginary people the author presents in a story. You can figure out what a character is like by noticing the author's description. You can also find out about characters by what they say and do and by what other characters say about them.

Setting: the time and place of a story

Narrator: the person who tells the story. If the narrator tells the story in the first person, the words "I" or "me" are used because everything is seen through the narrator's eyes. A first-person narrator can only tell about what he or she experiences or sees. A third-person narrator is not an actual character but usually tells the story as an outsider observing all the characters.

Following is an actual passage written in the third person from *Encyclopedia Brown and the Case of the Dead Eagles*:

Encyclopedia 's quick mind was in demand wherever he went. Not only did he solve cases at the dinner table, but often he was called upon to clear up a mystery when he least expected.

If this passage were written in the first person,

as if Encyclopedia were telling the story himself, the passage would read like this:

My quick mind was in demand wherever I went. Not only did I solve cases at the dinner table, but often I was called upon to clear up a mystery when I least expected.

Conflict: the struggle or problem the characters face
Rising Action: the buildup of events, struggles, and problems which the main character has to face
Climax: the turning point and most exciting part of the story or play
Falling Action or Resolution: the solving of the main character's problems

As you become a more experienced book-report writer, you will begin to feel comfortable using these terms in your reports. You will find other literary terms starting on page 74 in Chapter 5.

Reading Nonfiction
To get the most out of reading a book of nonfiction, take notes on the nonfiction bookmark note sheet shown on pages 10 and 11 and familiarize yourself with these sections before you begin your page-by-page reading of this kind of book.

Table of Contents: a listing of chapters and their pages located at the front of a nonfiction book. The Table of Contents not only gives you page numbers of each chapter but also provides you with an outline of what the whole book contains. Always study the Table of Contents carefully before you begin reading a book of nonfiction. Then skim it each time you start a new chapter. Doing this will only take a few seconds, yet it will help you preview what is coming up, review what you have already read, and help you remember old information and fit in new facts.

Headings: large, heavy-type titles at the beginning of a chapter and within it. Headings organize information for the reader, highlight the main ideas, and break up the information into manageable sections. Read over headings before and after you read a chapter to fix the information in your mind.

Captions, Graphs, Illustrations: visual aids that accompany and support the most important information. These aids help you picture complicated ideas. Take the time to look these over, since they will help you remember what you have read.

Index: an alphabetical listing in the back of a nonfiction book that tells you where to find specific information. Use the index to look up items you want to check or include in your book report.

As you read a nonfiction book, ask yourself whether the author explains the information clearly to you. In a biography or an autobiography, does the narrator help you get a picture of what the person was really like?

No matter what kind of book you read for your report, stay involved in your reading by taking notes and asking yourself: What is the author trying to say? Is the author being clear? What is going to happen next?

3
Write Up

Getting Organized

What happens after you finish a terrific book and have the notes to prove it? How do you get those great ideas out of your head and your notes onto a piece of paper? What does your teacher want, anyway?

Breathe easy. If your teacher has assigned a typical book report, he or she will probably want to see an explanation of your notes and thoughts grouped into these four areas:

1. one or two opening paragraphs that give a *summary* of what the book is about

2. another paragraph or two stating the *author's main idea*

3. a paragraph discussing one *special feature* of the book, such as the characters, the setting, the action, or the author's style

4. a conclusion expressing *your opinion* of the book.

If you took notes on the bookmark note sheet as you did your reading, you now have a ready-made outline of main ideas and supporting ideas to develop in your first draft. Now suppose you didn't get around to taking notes. First, promise yourself you will for the next book report. Then turn back to pages 8-11 and take notes now while the book is fresh in your mind. Follow the format shown on the bookmark note sheet or use the outline form shown on page 68 to organize your notes.

Writing
Step 7: Write your first draft.
If you have followed the recommended schedule, you should have several days or more left to work on your paper. Plan to spend most of that time writing the first draft. Working on the rough draft gives you a chance to try out different ways of saying something and make corrections *before* your teacher does.

Start off by writing on a clean sheet of paper the four numbered headings from your bookmark note sheet: *1. Summary, 2. Author's Main Idea, 3. Special Feature, 4. Opinion.* Leave plenty of space between each heading. Then, using information from your notes, develop a paragraph or two under each heading.

Here is what you need to know about each section of a standard book report. The examples discussed are based on a fictional book, *A Little Princess*, and a nonfiction book, *The Kids' Cat Book*. At the end of the chapter, you will find two sample book reports organized according to the four-part plan.

1. Summary: A well-written summary is like a book jacket that makes you want to read a book. It not only describes the main events or facts of the book, but it also gives the reader a feeling of what the book is like — funny, bittersweet, exciting, fascinating, suspenseful. An effective summary teases the reader a little by mentioning examples from the book that will make the reader want to read more. Here are a few tips to help you write the best possible summary.

• Think of your opening paragraph as a headline that has to grab the reader's attention. You can *startle* the reader like this: "Stop thinking your cat is lazy! According to *The Kids' Cat Book*, *all* cats sleep two thirds of the time. This book will also tell you why a cat's nose is like a human fingerprint and how many times a cat laps up liquid before it swallows."

You can also get your reader involved by asking

a *question:* "What would it be like to be raised almost as a princess, then lose everything you had?" You can also *sum up* a lot of information in an opener like this: "When seven-year-old Sara Crewe arrives at Miss Minchin's London boarding school from India, her trunks of velvet and lace dresses, her pony, her French maid, her china doll, Emily, and her handsome father, Captain Crewe, all seem to belong to someone who could only be a princess."

• Except for biographies, use the present tense to make your report seem immediate and alive.

• Be an authority by being direct. Avoid saying: "This book is about . . . " or "I think that . . ." or "In this report, I am going to discuss . . ." Instead, plunge right in with a direct statement: "If you have ever wondered about whether cats make good pets, *The Kids' Cat Book* is sure to convince you they do."

• Be specific. Weave in examples from the book to summarize the story or the information. In the previous example for *A Little Princess*, the reader learns that Sara Crewe is a wealthy seven-year-old from India, the daughter of a captain, and a new student at a boarding school in London. All this information is included as part of the main point: that Sara has everything a true princess would have.

• Don't give away the ending in your summary.

A good summary should tease the reader. To do this in your report, wind up the summary portion by mentioning some conflicts that come up without saying how the author works them out: "Find out what happens when Sara loses her father, her wealth, and her favored position at Miss Minchin's to become a lowly scullery maid." Or "Learn how Sara is rescued from her miserable life at Miss Minchin's by a mysterious person who has been watching her from afar."

In a nonfiction book, you might wind up the summary section of your report by saying something like this: "*The Kids' Cat Book* will tell you whether cats watch television, have dreams, or really do land on their feet when they fall long distances." In this way, you arouse the reader's curiosity without giving the entire book's contents away.

- Check that your summary section mentions:
  — the names of the main characters and a descriptive word or phrase about each one
  — a description of the setting
  — the conflict or problem the main characters face
  — the high point of the story
  — a hint about the ending of the book.

2. *Author's Main Idea:* In the middle section of your report, tell the reader what you think the writer is trying to get across. This is a little different

from telling what the book is about. Most writers hope that their readers will learn, experience, or understand certain feelings, ideas, or information. What do you think the author is trying to get at? In *A Little Princess*, the author seems to be saying that a young person can lose everything but still keep her pride.

Even a nonfiction book like the one about cats has a "big idea." The author's use of cat jokes, fascinating facts, and loving illustrations all suggest to the reader that cats make interesting, fun pets.

Here is a tip that will keep your reader interested in the middle section of your book report:

• Use quotations or examples from the book that you think express the author's main idea. "Over and over, Frances Hodgson Burnett says that having dreams helps a person survive: 'One of her *pretends* was that Emily was a good kind of witch who could protect her.' "

3. *Special Feature:* Every reader has a different way of looking at a book. Are you someone who gets more involved with the characters than the plot? Or is the action of a story the best part of a book for you? In a third section of your report, pick out one part of the book that affected you the most. "Frances Hodgson Burnett describes places in a way that makes you feel you are right there with Sara Crewe. 'It was not until long afterward that she realized that her bed had been so hard that

she turned over and over in it to find a place to rest, that the darkness seemed more intense than any she had ever known, and that the wind howled over the roof among the chimneys like something which wailed aloud.' ''

Again, back up your ideas by including one or two examples, facts, or quotations from the book to convince the reader that the special features you noticed — plot, characters, setting, or style — make the book worth reading or avoiding.

4. *Your Opinion:* This is your big windup and a chance to tell another reader just what you think of the book you read. Do you like the book because one of the characters is like you or someone you know? Is the book so exciting you had to keep turning the pages just to see what new surprises you would find? Are the facts in a nonfiction book so interesting that you got even more interested in the subject of the book? Even if you don't recommend the book, be sure to back up your opinion with examples from it. Your conclusion should leave your reader with the satisfied feeling that you have tied all your ideas together, whether you liked the book or not.

Following are a couple of writing tips to help you tie everything together at the end of your report:

• Try to echo the opening sentence of your report in the last sentence: ''Reading *The Kids' Cat Book* will help you see that your cat is normal, not lazy, when he spends most of his time sleeping." Or: "The facts and funny cat stories in *The Kids' Cat Book* will make you want to own a cat if you don't have one, or enjoy the cat you do have."

• Consider ending with a quotation from the book that sums up the main idea you have discussed in your report: "Above all, a reader will learn that holding on to your pride and your own thoughts will get you through terrible experiences. As Sara says, 'Whatever comes cannot alter one thing. If I am a princess in rags and tatters, I can be a princess inside.' "

Revising and Editing

Steps 8 and 9: Revise and proofread your first draft, then recopy your paper into a final draft.

Don't worry if your first draft looks like last week's shopping list. A rough draft is *supposed* to have words crossed out or inserted, scribbles, and chicken scratches all over. Your first draft is a tryout that gives you a chance to make changes ahead of time.

Have a colored pencil or marker on hand and maybe a dictionary and thesaurus. Clip the Editing Sheet on pages 70-73 of this book and check off the instructions listed there as you read through your rough draft and make revisions.

To make the actual changes, use the Proofreading

Sheet on page 69. These special markings show you how to add new words, take out old ones, and switch around sentences and paragraphs.

Once you feel confident that you have made all the changes you want, cross out the numbered headings on the rough draft. If you still have a day or two left on your schedule, put your report away overnight, then go back to it the next day. A break like this will help you see your paper in a new way when you reread it. You may have one or two more ideas to add or change when you see your rough draft again.

The next day, recopy your draft onto a clean sheet of paper by connecting all four sections, minus the headings. Then do a quick run-through to make sure you have corrected everything you intended to fix. Be sure you have included the book title, author's name, and your own name on the paper. (For examples of a fiction and a nonfiction book report, see pp. 34-38.)

Step 10: Turn your paper in on the due date.

Congratulations! You have written a terrific report. Put it into your book bag or notebook, so that you can turn it in right on time.

BOOK REPORT

Leslie O'Connor   April 30, 1988

A Little Princess
by Frances Hodgson Burnett

Fiction

What would it be like to be raised almost as a princess, then lose everything you had? That happens to seven-year-old Sara Crewe, who travels from India to Miss Minchin's strict London boarding school. Because of her trunks of velvet and lace dresses, her pony, her French maid, her expensive doll, Emily, and her handsome father, Captain Crewe, all the girls think of Sara as a princess. She isn't a real one, but she feels like one inside — proud, polite, and confident. Soon, all Miss Minchin's pupils, except for one or two jealous girls, want to be her friend.

Then, when Sara is ten, her life changes overnight. News comes of her father's death and the loss of their fortune. Cruel Miss Minchin immediately turns against Sara and forces her to become a maid in the school. A bossy and jealous girl named Lavinia enjoys seeing Sara in rags and living in a freezing attic. Except for Ermengarde, a lonely pupil struggling with school, and Becky, another servant girl, Sara is friendless. Yet she never stops believing in herself. The end of the book shows what happens when a mysterious stranger helps her become like a princess again.

Frances Hodgson Burnett, the author of *A Little Princess*, seems to be saying that hanging on to your dreams will help you survive anything. Even in her worst days living in the attic at Miss Minchin's, Sara dreams that clouds are beautiful objects, that ordinary food is a feast, and that her doll, Emily, is someone who is watching over her. "One of her *pretends* was that Emily was a good kind of witch who could protect her."

I like the way the author helps you picture what Sara's life is like when she is rich and when she is poor. "There were velvet dresses trimmed with costly furs, and lace dresses, and embroidered ones, and hats with great, soft ostrich feathers, and ermine coats and muffs, and boxes of tiny gloves, and handkerchiefs and silk stockings." Then the author describes Sara when she is poor. "... her shabby clothes were damp through. The absurd old feathers on her forlorn hat were more bedraggled and absurd than ever, and her downtrodden shoes were so wet that they could not hold any more water."

Watching how someone can go from being rich to being like a servant really made me want to keep reading. I like the way Sara Crewe never really gives up on herself, no matter how poor she is or how mean people are to her. The book made me realize that what you are inside is what counts. As Sara says: "Whatever comes cannot alter one thing. If I am a princess in rags and tatters, I can be a princess inside." Reading this book is a good way to learn how to believe in yourself, no matter what happens.

BOOK REPORT

Corey MacKenzie   April 30, 1988

The Kids' Cat Book
by the editors of *Owl Magazine*

Nonfiction

Stop thinking your cat is lazy! According to *The Kids' Cat Book*, *all* cats sleep two thirds of the time. This book will also tell you why a cat's nose is like a human fingerprint and how many times a cat laps up liquid before it swallows. There are kids' paintings of cats, a couple of poster-sized cat photos you could frame, and dozens of other photographs of cats doing everything from having kittens to giving themselves a bath. There are cartoon cats in comic strips and famous cats like Morris, Garfield, and the Pink Panther. Even noncat owners will laugh when they read some of the cat jokes: "What do cats read? Mewspapers!"

The book is filled with great facts about cats. *The Kids' Cat Book* will tell you whether cats watch television, have dreams, or really do land on their feet when they fall long distances.

The people who put together this book must really be cat lovers. They show the funny side of cats with jokes, puzzles, cartoons, and cat stories. The book also has an amazing story about a handicapped cat who wins a cat show. For noncat owners, there's a section of beautiful drawings of wild cats like lions, cheetahs, and leopards. All the information is so interesting and positive, the authors turn the readers into cat lovers, too.

I found this book funny and useful. Cat owners will find out all about breeding or choosing a cat, then get practical information about caring for it. A section called *Cat-log* is a cat scrapbook, designed like a baby book, for proud cat owners to complete.

No cat owner should be without this book. The facts and funny cat stories in *The Kids' Cat Book* will make you want to own a cat if you don't have one, or enjoy the cat you do have.

4
All Kinds of
Special Book Reports

Once you become a whiz at writing the kind of book report described in Chapter 3, your teacher may give you a chance to report on books in a different way. Every now and then, teachers encourage their students to share their reactions to books in oral book reports. Others like to advertise good books by having students illustrate books for reading displays. Occasionally, your teacher may assign a group of students to report on one book as if they were members of a panel. And once in a while, your teacher will leave it up to you to create your own special kind of book report.

Whether you want to create a musical version of a book you have read or design a completely new book jacket, you will still get the most out of your reading if you follow several of the same steps for writing a standard report: write down the assignment and due date; choose at least two books; plan a schedule for reading and notetaking. However, you may need to leave yourself more "hands-on" time for special reports that require materials such as audiovisual equipment, instruments, assistants, recordings, paintings, and so forth.

Special book reports require special ways of thinking about a book. If you read a book about a Native American, such as Forrest Carter's *The Education of Little Tree*, you could research information about the Cherokee tribe and create illustrations or models of that tribe's dress, dwellings, totems, and so forth. If your book takes place in the past, research information about what life was like for kids your age in that time period.

Have you ever seen a program called *Reading Rainbow*? For a book by Mary Calhoun called *Hot Air Henry*, which is about a cat who stows away on a hot air balloon, the program showed viewers how a hot air balloon works. *Gila Monsters Meet You at the Airport* by Marjorie Sharmat is not about gila monsters but about a city boy in the East who doesn't want to move out West, where he imagines giant lizards crawling everywhere. However, the *Reading Rainbow* show was about — you guessed it — gila monsters. So think about writing a nonfiction report on some aspect of a fictional book. A report on dugout houses would make an interesting companion to Laura Ingalls Wilder's *On the Banks of Plum Creek*. A paper on real-life detective techniques would add another dimension to any of the *Encyclopedia Brown* mysteries.

For a nonfiction book, the most obvious project would be some kind of display or demonstration of the book's information. However, you could also consider working that information into a children's fiction book of your own creation. For example, in a young children's fiction book called *Little Whale*, the author, Ann McGovern, presents facts about whales as she follows the main character, Little Whale, on its undersea journeys. The author also includes extra facts about whales on the inside cover. Another young children's book, *The Magic School Bus Inside the Earth*, features a fictional teacher and her students on a wild and hilarious class trip to the inside of the earth. Along the way, the author presents the kinds of facts readers are more used to seeing in an encyclopedia than in a storybook. Working in facts from a nonfiction book into a story of your own creation is a great way to get readers hooked on the information you have learned.

Whether you want to bring your golden retriever into class for a talk on *Old Yeller* or your pet rats for a discussion on *Mrs. Frisby and the Rats of N.I.M.H.*, make sure you get the go-ahead from your teacher on what you are allowed to do.

Focus on Oral Book Reports

Nothing makes most students come down with odd aches and pains like the prospect of an oral book report. Students worry about forgetting what they meant to say, running out of things to say, or stammering their way through the report.

How can you get more comfortable when you have to give an oral report? Here are some easy tips:

• Pick a book you really care about. When you have an oral book report coming up, spend more time than usual choosing the right book. In fact, choose three or four books from the library that seem to be surefire hits. If you have trouble staying interested in a book, you will have even more trouble talking about it.

• As with all other book reports, take notes on the bookmark note sheet as you go along. You will need plenty of facts and quotations so that you can give your listeners a very specific taste of what your book is about. Write down page numbers of passages you might want to read aloud during your report. Then before the report, mark those pages with scraps of paper so that you can open to them smoothly during your report.

• Organize your thoughts according to the form suggested in Chapter 3: *summary*, *author's main idea*, *special feature*, and *your opinion*. But instead of writing out the report completely, just put one heading on each card, and two or three phrases that sum up what you want to say. On the card, also write down page numbers for any quotations or passages you want to read so that you will bring the book to life for the class.

• If you feel comfortable writing out your report completely and then reading it, follow the book report format suggested in Chapter 3. However, do include a lively reading of the most exciting passages you can find to back up your ideas. Again, mark such pages with scraps of paper so that you can find these sections quickly. When you write up a report that you will be reading before the class, use every other line on the paper so that you can follow your sentences easily. Look up from your paper frequently in order to make eye contact with your audience. This will make your report seem more conversational.

• Whether you use note cards or a completely written-out report, plan a definite opening statement and conclusion. While you can ad lib in the middle, your opener and ending will create the most lasting impressions. So give yourself plenty of time to work on these sections.

• Regardless of whether you speak from note cards or an actual paper, do include a few sentences early on that tell the audience what the plot is about, where the story takes place, and who the characters are. Your listeners need an overall picture of the book so that they can fit in the specific information you mention later on. Before you begin the main part of your report, consider listing the title, author, and a few words about each character on the blackboard. Then you can point or refer to these as you get to them in the rest of your oral report.

• Practice your report in front of a mirror, with someone from your family, or on a tape recorder. This is the best way to "hear" the report in your mind.

• Don't be afraid to pause as you speak. Pauses will give you time to gather your thoughts and check your note cards or paper for the clues to your main point. Keep in mind that it's better to pause than to fill up the air with a lot of "ums" and "hmms."

• To connect your thoughts and help you move smoothly from one idea to the next, use connecting words or phrases such as "first," "second," "next," "finally," "on the other hand," "meanwhile," "in addition," "for instance." These words and expressions help you avoid the dreaded "and then."

• Speak slower and a little louder than you normally do. In their nervousness, many speakers rush through what they want to say. Don't worry about boring your audience by speaking slowly. Remember, for an oral report, you will be doing more reading from the book than you would in a written report. Authors such as Sid Fleischman and Beverly Cleary won't bore your audience.

• Use props to steady those fidgety hands. The best prop is the book itself. Hold up the cover for everyone to see. Open up to any illustrations and comment on them. Bring in picture books that tie into the setting of your book. Remember to mark such places in the book with slips of paper so that you can turn to them easily.

• Consider using costumes, music, or sound effects to recreate the setting or mood of the book. Ask your teacher ahead of time if you can darken the classroom for a report on a horror or mystery story.

• Use the blackboard as a prop to write down main points you want your audience to notice. Then point to them as you move along in your report. Many speakers and teachers do just that when they speak.

• Ask your teacher if you can pair off with a partner or several other students to present a group report, with each of you reporting on one part of the book you particularly like. That way you spread out the nervousness *and* share the glory!

• Open up with something startling to get your audience's attention right away. Ask a good question: "Have you ever wondered what might happen if you opened your closet and found that it led to a secret passage?" Or make a wild statement: "Anybody who's afraid of ghosts should avoid reading this book." Read an exciting, funny, sad, or very descriptive passage from the book as your opener, then go on to describe why that section is typical of what the reader will find in the book. If you are reporting on a book with a surprise ending, begin by summarizing the plot to the high point of the book, then ask your classmates to guess what happens at the end.

• Leave time for your audience to ask questions. Even nervous speakers relax more when they answer specific questions. If you think people won't raise their hands, ask your own questions, then answer them. For example, you might wind up by saying something like this: "Now some of you might be asking, how does the author get you to believe that an elevator keeps rising and lands in another time and place?" Then go on to discuss how that happens in the book.

• Plan a definite windup that sums up your opinions. If you trail off, so will your audience. End with a smile, knowing you did your best.

• Most town libraries have summer reading contests that encourage you to read a certain number of books and then report on them to the librarian. A lot of these contests feature prizes such as special T-shirts, certificates, badges, and other bonuses.

Giving these short reports to the librarian, with no audience other than the two of you, is a terrific way to practice speaking about books without using any notes. You may even win a complete set of dinosaur stickers or twenty-two ice-cream-cone coupons!

Activities

• Tape your oral book report and donate it to the school library.

• Have a partner videotape your review of a book that you liked or hated. Make sure you use some visual props to liven up your report.

• Team up with a classmate to present two opposing, or different, views of a book you have both read.

• Write a radio or television commercial selling the book to the audience. Use props, visual aids, and taped sound effects to make your commercial convincing.

• Open your oral report with a short summary of the book, then turn to your favorite passage, read it aloud, and tell the class why you chose it.

• Write up a list of questions directed to the author or a character in the book. Then have your teacher or a partner ask you these questions, which you will answer as if you were the author or character. As an alternative, ask yourself these questions on a tape recorder, then answer them as if you were the author or character being interviewed for a talk on the radio.

• Imagine yourself as a salesperson for the publisher of the book you read. Try to convince booksellers to stock the book in their stores. Make up flyers or a sheet listing the book's selling points to strengthen your sales pitch.

Focus on the Author:
Writing Topics and Activities

• Research the life of the author of the book you have read and write a minibiography of that person.

• Imagine that the author of the book you read is visiting your school. Make up a list of questions you would like him or her to answer for you and other readers.

• If the author is still alive, write a letter to him or her asking how he or she got the idea for the book. Usually, readers send such letters to the publisher, who then forwards the letter to the writer. Don't be disappointed if you don't get an answer, though. Popular writers get so much mail, they can't always respond to everyone. But it's worth a try!

• Discuss what you think is the author's most important message in the book. Do you agree or disagree with this view?

• If you have read more than one book by the author, write a report in which you compare the books. Or team up with someone who has read a different book by the same author and give an oral report to the class comparing each of your reactions to the books.

Focus on Plot:
Writing Topics and Activities

• What is the opening scene of the plot? Tell why it did or didn't interest you enough to continue reading on.

• What is the problem the main characters have to face? How do the characters solve this problem?

• Write a "Dear Abby" letter from one of the main characters in which he or she asks for advice on solving his or her main problem. Then answer the letter.

• What is the climax or turning point of the book? How do the characters and situations change after the turning point?

• Describe the ending of the book. Discuss whether the ending was satisfying or not. In what other ways might the book have ended?

• Discuss whether the plot was believable, suspenseful, or interesting enough to keep you turning the pages.

• Write a new ending to the book.

• On poster-sized paper, draw a time line of the main events of the book.

• Create a board game in which the spaces on the game are events in the plot, the markers are the main characters, and the cards are large and small problems which the characters face. Borrow markers from board games you have at home and use simple games such as Candyland or the Enchanted Forest as models for developing game rules and strategies for your own board game.

• Create a comic book or a comic strip page that features a major scene from the book in each box.

• Design a bookmark or book jacket for the book that describes the plot in 100 words or less.

Focus on Characters:
Writing Topics and Activities

• Choose your favorite character in the book and discuss why you chose that person.

• Discuss how you think the author feels toward one of the main characters. For example, do you think the author is sympathetic, friendly, disapproving, or loving toward the character?

• What is the main character's most significant speech or action in the book? Discuss why you think so.

• Write a diary entry from the point of view of

one of the main characters which covers an important event in that character's life.

• Create a new character for the book and describe how that character would fit in with the others, and how the existing characters would react to this new person.

• Find a book of astrology and choose a sign that best fits each of the main characters. Give reasons for your choice.

• Draw or paint a picture of what you imagine one of the main characters would look like. Consider drawing a caricature, an exaggerated portrait, of any character who has unusual or strong traits.

• Turn one of the main characters into a superhero and create an abridged or shortened version of the book.

• Invite the characters from the book to a theme party. Design invitations, plan the foods to be served and the gifts to be given to each character. Discuss real-life or other fictional characters from other books whom you would also invite to your party. Write up a gossip-column-style description of the party as you think it would have taken place.

Focus on Setting:
Writing Topics and Activities

• Describe the most memorable settings in the book and discuss why you think they were important.

• Discuss how changing the setting — for example, the time or place — might affect the characters and events of the book. If your book takes place in the past, how would you envision the same people in today's world?

• Imagine you are a designer who has been asked to create a set for a scene from the book or a room for one of the characters. Discuss how you would make these scenes look.

• Illustrate a major location from the book based on the author's description of it.

• Build a model of a setting from the book from scrap lumber, or use a shoebox, found objects, and your imagination to design and build a diorama of an important setting.

• Make a collage of objects and printed words from newspapers and magazines that give the viewer a feeling for the mood of the book.

• In drawings and paintings, create a set for one of the scenes from the book or design a room for one of the characters.

• If your book takes place in an unusual or exotic

setting, illustrate and write a travel brochure describing that location.

• Create a new book cover that illustrates the book's setting.

Focus on Mysteries:
Writing Topics and Activities

• Write a newspaper article about the crime that occurred in the book, then write a follow-up article about the solution to the crime.

• Write up a summary of the mystery, along with suggestions of how it might be filmed. Imagine you are sending this proposal to a television network to consider as a TV movie or the pilot of a mystery series.

• Write down all the important clues from the book on the board and ask classmates to guess what the crime might have been. Follow up by summarizing the mystery without giving away the solution. Ask students how they think the mystery was solved, telling which students came closest to the real ending without giving it away.

Focus on Science Fiction:
Writing Topics and Activities

• Write a detailed description of the kind of world in which the story takes place.

• Describe why you would or would not want to live in the unusual places or times described in the book.

• Discuss how the beings in the book are similar or dissimilar to humans.

• Describe the unusual problems or situations that are special to the world described in the book.

• Illustrate any unusual places or creatures in the story to help readers envision it.

• Create clay models of places or beings particular to the book.

• Make a science-fiction poster advertising the book.

Focus on Romance:
Writing Topics and Activities

• Write a love letter one of the characters might have written to another but was too shy to mail.

• Create a dating questionnaire and fill it out for each of the main characters in the book. List questions that will help the characters discuss their interests, likes and dislikes, appearance, and what that person might be looking for in another person.

• Write a new ending to the book that ends in the opposite way of the actual ending.

Focus on Supernatural, Horror, and Occult Books:
Writing Topics and Activities

• Write a newspaper account of some of the unusual events in the book.

• Write a radio-play version of the book, complete with sound effects and music. If possible, perform the radio play for the class, either live or on tape.

• Do a reading of a particularly spooky passage in the book. To heighten the atmosphere, seat everyone in a circle, darken the room, and use startling sound effects and music that you have taped beforehand.

• Imagine yourself as a scientist who has been asked to explain the unusual events in the book. Write up a report in a scientific style.

Focus on Plays:
Writing Topics and Activities

• In a written or an oral report, quote the most memorable lines from the play and explain why they are important.

• In a written or an oral report, explain why you would like to see a performance of the play you have read.

• Imagine you are the producer of the play and your job is to make a one-minute commercial for the play. Organize several students to act out a scene that might make a viewer or listener want to see the rest of the play. You may choose to do this live before the class or on tape.

Focus on Poetry:
Writing Topics and Activities

• Choose your favorite poem from the collection you have read and discuss why you chose it.

• Compare two poems on the same subject and discuss how the poets express their ideas similarly or differently.

• Discuss what images or word pictures the poet uses in a favorite poem to make you experience certain feelings.

• Select three or four poems from the collection that you particularly like, copy them down, then illustrate them in a way that conveys the feelings of each one. Read these poems to the class and share your illustrations.

• Write your own poem in response to one of the poems you enjoyed.

• Memorize a poem that you think the class would enjoy and recite it to the class.

Focus on Autobiography and Biography:
Writing Topics and Activities

• Write a report discussing why the subject of the book you read is worth reading about.
• Write a report in which you focus on what the subject's life was like when he or she was the age you are now.
• Write a report in which you discuss the obstacles and problems the subject faced and overcame.
• Find a written or spoken quotation by the subject and discuss how this passage shows you something important about the person.
• If this person were alive today, what questions would you want to ask him or her? List the questions and discuss how you think that person might have answered them.
• Talk or write about the person's greatest strength and greatest weakness.
• Prepare a time line of the major events in the subject's life and use it to give a talk about that person.
• Discuss what you learned in the biography or autobiography that might help you in your own life now or later on.

• Share any photographs or illustrations included in the book you read and see if you can track down other illustrations in various books. Use these pictures as a visual aid for discussing the person you read about.

Focus on Nonfiction:
Writing Topics and Activities

• Discuss three questions you had about the subject of the book before you read it and how the book did or did not answer them.

• Name five important new facts you learned and why you think they are important.

• If the book you read is a "how-to" or "self-help" book, discuss whether you think the advice it offered is worthwhile.

• Discuss what kind of reader would most enjoy the book you read.

• Find as many illustrations or photographs as you can on the subject of the book. Then use them as visual aids in an oral report about the subject.

• If the nonfiction book you read contains experiments or explains how to do something, gather the necessary materials and perform the experiment or procedure for the class.

• Bring in objects, souvenirs, or collections you have that tie into the subject of your book. Use these to introduce or explain the information in the book.

Focus on Group Reports

• With other students who have read the same book, plan a bulletin board display for the classroom or hallway. One student can work on a plot summary, another can write about characters or setting. One or two students can write book reviews or select and discuss special passages from the book. Each group member should contribute one artistic piece — a new book cover, bookmark, poster, banner, or an illustration to accompany the written pieces. Arrange the writing and artwork under a colorful heading announcing the book.

• Four or five students who have read the same book can form a panel in which each member discusses just one part of the book the group has read.

• Make up some serious and silly book awards like: Most Exciting Plot, Character I Would Most Like to Meet, Book Most Likely to Put You to Sleep. Then hold an awards ceremony in which each student nominates his or her book for one of the awards. The teacher will decide on winners based on how effectively individual students argue for their book.

A Grab Bag of Book Report Projects

• Create a puzzle which a reader should be able to complete after reading the book.

• Write an original poem inspired by the book you have read.

• Make up a vocabulary list of difficult words in the book and write down their definitions.

• Make up a test consisting of questions a student should be able to answer after reading the book.

• Write a book review for a magazine directed to middle schoolers.

• Write a letter recommending the book to someone your age.

• Make a mobile for the classroom that shows different parts of the book. At the top of the mobile, write the title and author of the book. On the reverse side of that piece, draw a small picture of something that gives the feeling of the book. Then label six or seven different-shaped pieces with the words "setting," "character," "plot" (use as many pieces as you need for each). Draw a picture on the reverse side of each piece that shows something about the setting, characters, and events in the plot. String the pieces together and hang them from a hanger for classroom display.

5
Book Report Kit

Ten Steps to A+ Book Reports

Step 1: Write down everything you need to know about the assignment.

Step 2: Visit the library or bookstore right away and choose at least two books.

Step 3: Plan a daily reading and writing schedule.

Step 4: Read a little every day.

Step 5: Take notes as you read.

Step 6: Organize your notes.

Step 7: Write your first draft.

Step 8: Revise and proofread your first draft.

Step 9: Recopy your paper into a final draft.

Step 10: Turn your paper in on the due date.

BOOK REPORT SCHEDULE AND CHECKLIST

Jobs to be done	Due Date	Completed
1. Get the assignment.	_____	_____
2. Get at least two books.	_____	_____
3. Finish reading and notetaking.	_____	_____
4. Organize notes.	_____	_____
5. Finish first draft.	_____	_____
6. Correct first draft.	_____	_____
7. Recopy first draft into final draft.	_____	_____
8. Complete report and turn it in.	_____	_____

Book Guides

Stumped for a good book to read? Check the reference section of your library to see if any of the following book guides, or any others, are available. Books guides usually group titles by subject, then alphabetically by title. The entries often include a brief plot summary or description of the book to help you decide if you will like it.

Carlsen, G. Robert, editor, *Books and the Teenage Reader*, Bantam, 1980.

Cullinan, Bernice, and M. Jerry Weiss, editors, *Books I Read When I Was Young*, Avon Books, 1980.

National Council of Teachers of English, *Your Reading, A Booklist for Junior High and Middle School Students*, 1983.

Petersen, Linda Kauffman, and Marilyn Leathers Solt, *Newbery and Caldecott Medal Honor Book*, G.K. Hall & Co., 1982.

Spirt, Diana L., *Introducing Bookplots 3, A Book Talk Guide for Use with Readers Ages 8-12*. R. R. Bowker Company, 1988.

```
┌─────────────────────────────────────────────┐
│                 (Side 1)                    │
│           BOOKMARK NOTE SHEET               │
│                 Fiction                     │
├─────────────────────────────────────────────┤
│ Title:                                      │
├─────────────────────────────────────────────┤
│ Author:                                     │
├─────────────────────────────────────────────┤
│ Date Book Was Published:                    │
├─────────────────────────────────────────────┤
│                                             │
│ 1. Summary                                  │
│     Main Characters:                        │
│     Name          A few words about them    │
│                                             │
│                                             │
│                                             │
│                                             │
│     Plot:                                   │
│     The book begins when                    │
│                                             │
│                                             │
│     Most of the story takes place (when and where) │
│                                             │
│                                             │
│     The main events and problems that happen are │
│                                             │
│                                             │
│     The story ends when                     │
│                                             │
│                                             │
└─────────────────────────────────────────────┘
```

(Side 1)

BOOKMARK NOTE SHEET

Fiction

Title:

Author:

Date Book Was Published:

1. Summary

    Main Characters:

    Name   A few words about them

    Plot:

    The book begins when

    Most of the story takes place (when and where)

    The main events and problems that happen are

    The story ends when

2. Author's Main Idea

    I think the author was trying to say that

○

    Page numbers of quotations that show the author's

main idea:

3. Special Feature

    One part of the book that makes it special (or weakens

it) is

○

    Page numbers of quotations that show this special

feature:

4. Your Opinion

    This book made me feel that

○   I would ___ would not ___ recommend this book because

    Other page numbers I might need:

(Side 1)	
BOOKMARK NOTE SHEET	
Nonfiction	

Title:

Author:

◯   Date Book Was Published:

1. Summary

    This book is about

2. Author's main idea

    The author thinks that

◯

    Page numbers of quotations that show the author's

    main idea:

3. Special feature

◯   One of the good/bad things about this book is that

    Page numbers of quotations or examples that show

    special feature:

(Side 2)

4. Opinion

This book helped me learn that
○

I would ___ would not ___ recommend this book because

Other page numbers I might need:
○

○

Outline Form

I. _____

   A. _____

      1. _____

      2. _____

   B. _____

      1. _____

      2. _____

   C. _____

      1. _____

      2. _____

II. _____

   A. _____

      1. _____

      2. _____

   B. _____

      1. _____

      2. _____

   C. _____

      1. _____

      2. _____

III. _____

   A. _____

      1. _____

      2. _____

   B. _____

Proofreading Sheet

Use these signs to make corrections on your rough draft as you read it out loud.

$\wedge$ This arrow shows where $\overset{TO}{\wedge}$add

a word, phrase, or punctuation mark.

$\equiv$ capitalize the word.

⌗   ⌗Start a new paragraph.

ℓ   Take out the extra word or words.

𝑁   Reverse the letters.

/   Split the words that are jammed together.

⊙   Add a period⊙

↗   Move this to a better place. (If you have

a whole paragraph to move, you may

want to cut apart your paper and rear-

range and tape it in a better order. You

can save time doing this instead of

recopying everything just to see how

the new arrangement looks.)

$\overset{\text{\textit{ll}}}{V}$ $\overset{\text{\textit{ll}}}{V}$ $\overset{\text{\textit{ll}}}{}$Add quotation marks, $\overset{\text{\textit{ll}}}{}$she said.

Editing Sheet

	Yes	Needs fixing

Summary:

1. My summary begins with an attention-getting sentence. _____ _____
2. I have mentioned the main characters and described them in a few words. (fiction) _____ _____
3. I have written about the main facts of the book. (nonfiction) _____ _____
4. I have said something about the setting of the story. (fiction) _____ _____
5. I have used examples, quotations, or facts from the book to back up my main ideas. _____ _____
6. I have mentioned the conflict the main character faces. (fiction) _____ _____

7. I have ended the summary section by giving hints about the most interesting parts of the book without giving it away. _____ _____

Author's Main Idea:
1. I have stated the author's main idea and backed it up with at least one fact, example, or quotation from the book. _____ _____

Special Feature:
1. I have discussed one part of the book that I especially noticed, such as the plot, action, setting, characters, or style. _____ _____
2. I have used at least one example that shows this special feature. _____ _____

Opinion:

1. I have told the reader what I think of the book and backed up my opinion with at least one example, fact, or quotation from the book. _____ _____

2. I have tried to end the report by: repeating the opening sentence in a new way; or raising a question that will make someone want to read (or avoid) the book; or ending with a direct quotation from the book. _____ _____

Grammar and style:

1. I have written my name, the date, the book title, author, and fiction or nonfiction at the top of my report. _____ _____

2. I have left a few spaces before all paragraphs. _____ _____

3. I have capitalized all sentences, names, places, and dates. _____ _____

4. I have ended each sentence with a period, question mark, or exclamation point. _____ _____

5. I have put a comma wherever I paused between ideas within a sentence. _____ _____

6. I have checked spelling I wasn't sure of. _____ _____

7. I have used quotation marks for all quotations from the book. _____ _____

Literary Terms

Allegory: a story in which the characters stand for a certain human quality or idea. Many fables like *The Fox and the Grapes* or *The Tortoise and the Hare* are allegories in which animals represent human traits.

Atmosphere: the mood or feeling of a story

Autobiography: a biography or story about one's own life

Biography: a true story written about another person's life

Characters: the imaginary people the author presents in a story

Characterization: the way an author presents a character

Climax: the turning point or most exciting part of the story

Conflict: the struggle or problem the characters face in a novel or play

Critique: a review of a book, play, movie, show, etc.

Drama: a work written for the stage, such as a play

Fable: a very short story, usually with animal characters, which teaches a lesson about human behavior

Falling action: the solving of the main character's problems in a fictional work

Fantasy: a work that contains supernatural happenings and beings

Fiction: books about made-up people and events

Flashback: a movement from the present time in a story or play to an event that happened in the past

Foreshadowing: a hint that some event will happen

Hero: a main character in a work who possesses positive qualities

Ideas: attitudes and feelings the author presents directly or indirectly in a book

Incident: an event that takes place in a story or play

Irony: a twist of words or events that turns out the opposite of what is expected

Legend: a popular story handed down from the past that may or may not be true

Mood: the feeling in a story, play, or poem

Myth: a story involving supernatural persons and events that often explains real events in history

Narrative: a story of related events

Narrator: the person who tells a story

Novel: a book-length story

Parable: a story with human characters that teaches a moral or lesson

Parody: a story, play, or poem that imitates, in a humorous way, a serious work

Plot: the chain of events in a story

Point of view: the way in which the author tells the story. A first-person narrator who tells a story in the first person is usually a character in a story and uses the words "I" or "me" because he sees everything through his eyes. A first-person narrator can only tell about what he experiences and sees himself. A third-person narrator is not an actual character in a story but seems to stand apart from the story, observing everything. This kind of narrator can describe thoughts and feelings of many characters.

Purpose: the author's goal in telling a story

Resolution: the solving of the main character's problems in a fictional work

Rising action: the build-up of events, struggles, and problems the main character has to face

Satire: a work that makes fun of human weaknesses

Setting: the time and place of a story

Style: an author's way of expressing himself or herself

Subplot: a second plot that is less important than the main plot

Symbol: a character, event, or object that stands for an idea

Theme: an author's major idea in a work

Villain: a wicked enemy of the hero

Character Interview Form

How would you like to be a famous character? Or have a favorite character step outside the book into real life? If you have an oral book report coming up, get a partner to ask you the questions on the following form and conduct an interview for the rest of the class.

Book title: _____

Author: _____

Character Interviewed: _____

Interviewer: How do you feel about the way you were presented in the book?
Character: _____
_____
_____

Interviewer: What was the most difficult problem you faced in the book?
Character: _____
_____
_____

Interviewer: What was going on in your mind during the most difficult moment in the story?
Character: _____
_____
_____

Interviewer: What were your feelings about some of the other characters in the book?

Character: _____

_____

_____

Interviewer: If the author were to rewrite this book, what changes do you wish he or she would make?

Character: _____

_____

_____

Interviewer: How do you feel about the way the book ended?

Character: _____

_____

_____

Interviewer: What would you like readers to know about you in addition to what they learned in the book?

Character: _____

_____

_____

Interviewer: Now that your work is complete in this book, what are your plans for the future?

Character: _____

_____

_____

File Card Book Report

_____
(title)

_____
(author)

_____
(reviewed by)

_____
(category)

Brief plot summary: _____

_____

Main characters and brief description: _____

_____

☐ I recommend this book because _____

☐ I do not recommend this book because _____

79

Reader's Scorecard Sheet

Title	Author	Date Read	Book Report Grade	Rating (Great, Good, Fair, Not Recommended)	Comments

Title	Author	Date Read	Book Report Grade	Rating (Great, Good, Fair, Not Recommended)	Comments

Title	Author	Date Read	Book Report Grade	Rating (Great, Good, Fair, Not Recommended)	Comments

Title	Author	Date Read	Book Report Grade	Rating (Great, Good, Fair, Not Recommended)	Comments

Index